JAKE PLUMMER

Comeback Cardinal

by

Steve Schoenfeld

SPORTS PUBLISHING INC.
www.SportsPublishingInc.com

©1999 Sports Publishing Inc.
All rights reserved.

Production manager: Susan M. McKinney
Series Editor: Rob Rains
Photo Coordinator: Claudia Mitroi
Cover design: Scot Muncaster and Todd Lauer
Photos: AP/Wide World Photos, Marilyn Plummer,
Joe Robbins, Brian Spurlock

ISBN: 1-58261-165-3
Library of Congress Catalog Card Number: 99-68304

SPORTS PUBLISHING INC.
www.SportsPublishingInc.com

Printed in the United States.

CONTENTS

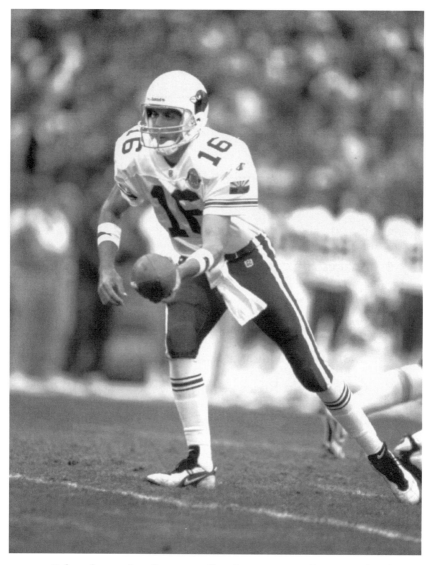

Jake always has been a take-charge type of quarterback.
(Joe Robbins)

1

Taking Charge

Jake "The Snake" Plummer didn't jog when he ran onto the field for his first NFL game. He sprinted—a sign that he was immediately in charge.

None of his Arizona Cardinals teammates had to ask him to speak up so they could hear him. His message was loud and clear.

"He said, 'Let's go 98 yards and win the game,'" recalled fullback Larry Centers.

Going 98 yards would be a daunting task. No NFL quarterback had taken his team more than 66 yards for a score on his first possession.

Cardinals Coach Vince Tobin had not planned on Jake beginning his pro career in that situation back in 1997. The game was in the hostile environment of Philadelphia's Veterans Stadium. Tobin had told Jake on the sideline that he would enter the game the next time the Cardinals got the ball. So what was he going to do? Tell the rookie to stay on the sideline just because the team had bad field position?

Tobin didn't flinch. He sent Jake onto the field early in the fourth quarter on October 19, 1997, not knowing what to expect. He knew Jake couldn't do much worse. Through three quarters, the Cardinals had been shut out and had accumulated only 94 yards of total offense.

It took only two plays for Jake to face his first big test. The Cardinals faced a third and two, and desperately needed a first down.

Jake, 6-foot-2, 197 pounds, scrambled around

right end for 5 yards and returned to an excited huddle.

"After Jake's scramble, I said to him, 'You're bad. You're a bad dude,'" Centers said.

"He says, 'Yeah, I am, aren't I?'"

"I thought, 'That cocky rookie.'"

Just as he predicted, Jake drove the Cardinals for a go-ahead score. They wound up losing, 13-10, in overtime, but a star was born.

"He has an aura about him that says, 'I'm going to be successful.'"

"I sat there during that (98-yard) drive thinking, 'Look at the poise. Look at his footwork and mechanics,'" veteran deep snapper Trey Junkin said.

Two years later, he's the most popular athlete in Arizona and the first quarterback to lead the Cardinals to an NFL playoff victory in 51 years.

Jake signed a four-year, $29.7-million contract extension in December 1998, which included an NFL-record $15 million signing bonus.

Jake (center) has two older brothers, Brett (left) and Eric. (Marilyn Plummer)

in the Wilderness

His name wasn't supposed to be Jake. He was supposed to be named "Jacqueline."

"I had two boys," his father, Steve, said. "We were hoping Jake would be a girl."

Instead, Steven and Marilyn Plummer had Jason Steven Plummer, who later would be called "Jake." They started calling him Jake after Buzz Cheatam and Jody Robb, who operated the Smiley Creek Lodge and paid him for odd jobs, including

The Plummer boys and their mother, Marilyn, enjoy a camping trip in the Sawtooth Mountains. (Marilyn Plummer)

filling salt and pepper shakers. They nicknamed him, "Jaker Baker the Money Maker."

"We have this one picture when he was real small," Jake's dad said. "He had his older brother's football uniform on. He had that page-boy, long, blond hair. Now, we look at that sometimes and shake our heads."

Jake had just turned three when the family moved from Boise, Idaho, to the tiny town of Smiley Creek (population 50) in the foothills of the Sawtooth Mountains. How tiny was the town? Jake's mother taught grade school in a two-room schoolhouse.

The weather was frigid in the winter. Jake can remember days when it was as cold as 40 below zero.

"It was fun there," Jake said. "It was great. We didn't have TV, Nintendo. I just had my bike and fishing pole. We made a couple of toys. I had to do

Jake learned to cross-country ski in the Sawtooth Mountains. (Marilyn Plummer)

with what I had.

"I just didn't go down to the roller-skating rink or to the nickel arcade. I had to make up my own games. There weren't many neighbors, just older people."

Jake learned to cross-country ski at an early age. He was a prodigy.

"He was watching free-style skiing on TV," his mom said. "Then, he put the skis on for the first time and said, 'Mom, when we ski today, I'm going to do flips.' There was never anything he didn't think he could do."

The family stayed a couple of years before his dad sold the place and the family moved back full time to Boise.

In Boise, Jake's brothers started a lawn-care business. Jake was only five at the time, too young to help. But he still was involved.

"Jake looked at his brothers' business cards and

(From left) Jake, Brett and Eric in 1992. (Marilyn Plummer)

said, 'Where's my business card?' his mother said.

"I said, 'Well, what do you do, Jake?'

Jake said, 'Well, I'm a good friend.'"

His mother had a business card made that said,

Jake gets off a pass for the Cardinals. (Joe Robbins)

CHAPTER THREE

Family Affair

Jake's parents were divorced when he was in the third grade. They remain close friends, maybe best friends.

"I didn't like it," Jake said of the divorce. "I missed my dad. I didn't get to see him that much until the summer. But I have to give my parents credit. They weren't going to let anything that came between them affect what I felt for my dad or my mom. I spent my summers with my dad. He came to a lot of my games during the rest of the year. We did all kinds of stuff together."

Jake had plenty of family around him. He was close to his 10 cousins, four of whom lived in California. He still refers to them as his "crazy cousins from California."

It is an interesting group. Jake's uncle, Norm Davis, his mom's brother, is a disc jockey. He has a show in Tampa, Florida, a blues show called "Midnight Flier" that he syndicates over the Internet.

Jake's cousin, Susie, Norm's oldest daughter, is considered the family rock star. She has played with Billy Idol, Prince, Mick Jagger and Van Morrison.

Another of Jake's cousins, Scott Davis, is a computer expert. Then, there is Scott's brother, Sean, who has a rock band, "The Transient Lemmings" and makes designs from stones.

"All of the others are real creative, too," Jake said. "We always made real fun movies growing up.

Whenever they came to town, we'd always make some films."

They also taught Jake pottery. He learned to build "monsters and freaky things" out of clay.

"I was (artistic) growing up," he said. "It's something I'd like to get back into. I used to draw a lot. I like pottery. I like to tap my creative side once in awhile."

*Jakes waves hello to family and friends at a press conference.
(AP/Wide World Photos)*

Snakes Alive

Jake "The Snake" likes his nickname, but he can't stand snakes. In fact, he hates them. If a snake came his way, he would run as if an opposing defender were chasing him.

That almost happened in 1996 when ABC-TV took him to "A" Mountain on the Arizona State campus to film a feature for its Rose Bowl pre-game show. They brought some snakes for props but almost didn't have Jake, then an ASU senior.

Jake and his dog, Willis, during Jake's rookie year.
(Marilyn Plummer)

There also was the time in 1995 when a six-year-old youngster found a six-inch garter snake near a creek in outside Payson, Arizona. He took the snake home to show it to his hero.

Jake wasn't impressed. "Get that thing away from me," Jake told him.

Fans have learned not to bring Jake reptiles. Instead, they bring him hats, shirts, shoes and cards to sign.

In April 1999, the demand for Jake's clinic was so great, people had to be turned away.

He showed the kids how to grip the football, how to throw with a quick release. Then, he talked to them about school, parents, eating the right foods, everything but snakes.

"I like animals—dogs, cats," Jake said. "But I don't like snakes. You never know when they're going to take a bite out of you.

Jake became a quarterback at the age of 11.
(Marilyn Plummer)

"I guess it's a funny thing—calling me 'The Snake,' and I don't like them."

His older brother, Eric, gets the credit for Jake being "The Snake." He gave him the nickname when Jake was in the seventh grade after Jake read former Oakland Raider quarterback Ken "The Snake" Stabler's autobiography.

Jake has been "The Snake" ever since.

Jake "The Snake" gets ready to take the snap from center Aaron Graham. (Joe Robbins)

Born to Run

Jake is not the only athlete in the family. His dad was one of the fastest kids in his high school.

"He has known my mom since they were 13 years old," Jake said. "My mom was real fast. My dad tells a story that he had a crush on my mom because she was the first girl who had ever beaten him in a foot race."

His mom tells a different story. "Actually, we tied."

Jake's dad became an accomplished handball player and his mom a successful racquetball player.

Jake's brothers still brag that they are superior athletes. "I couldn't beat them in anything growing up," Jake said. "Now, besides ping pong or pool, a couple of little games like that, I pretty much can beat them.

"I had great incentive trying to beat them. You always want to beat your older brother—shooting H-O-R-S-E out in the front yard. You get beat all your life. When the day comes and you finally beat your older brother in something, you feel like quite a man."

Jake's brother, Brett, now 30, was one of the top track stars in Boise. He set a junior high record in the 400 meters and a high school mark in the 4 by 400 relay.

Later, when Brett attended Brown University, he was one of the school's top distance runners, setting records in the 800 and 1,500 meters.

Eric, 27, was a handball player at the University of Montana.

They used to pick on Jake. "I used to beat up Eric, and he'd go and beat up Jake, and then I'd have to beat up Eric for beating up Jake," Brett said.

In the third grade, Jake told his mom he was going to be a running back in the NFL.

"All of his art projects, stories he wrote in grade school, were about playing in the NFL," his mom said.

Jake showed at an early age that he was an exceptional athlete. He was only nine when he played shortstop on a Little League team of 12-year-olds.

"I was bragging about him to my friends," Brett said. "They told me to quit bragging about him. Now, he's all they want to talk about."

At the age of nine, Jake played shortstop on a team made up of 12-year-olds.
(Marilyn Plummer)

When Jake was a sophomore, his high school basketball team won the regional championship.
(Marilyn Plummer)

Jake's mom didn't allow Brett and Eric to play youth football. She thought they would get hurt.

She relented when Jake asked to play. "I begged her so much, she pretty much let me do it to get me to shut up," Jake said.

Said his mother: "He and his friend followed me around a whole afternoon. Finally, I said, 'Fine. OK.'"

Jake's best friend (Casey Richards) in the fifth grade invited Jake to football practice so he could see what it was like. Jake then told his mother, "We play every day at recess and tackle each other without pads, and at least now I have pads."

Jake liked football so much, he once climbed to the roof of the family's house to adjust the antenna for "Monday Night Football." He read every book about football from the library.

When Jake was 11, he played in a youth football game which his father attended. He was so pumped up, he started crying. He still managed to make 21 tackles.

He was a receiver until the day he fired a strike back at his friend, Casey.

"The coach said, 'Wait a minute. Do that again,'" Jake's mother said. "The coach said he couldn't believe a nine-year-old could throw a perfect spiral, and he made him a quarterback.

"None of the kids could catch a spiral, so he had to show them how to handle one. Jake came to him after the switch and said, 'I'm not going to play quarterback because Casey wants to be quarterback.' And (the coach) just said, 'I'm the coach, and you're the quarterback; you do what I tell you to do.'

"They did flea flickers and everything. It was the most fun team to watch. All the dads were rolling on the ground laughing."

Jake was a three-sport star at Capital High School in Boise, also playing baseball and basketball.

He was a swingman in basketball. "I was just a hustler," Jake said. "I'd get loose balls. I'd play defense. That was my strength."

Jake's high school teammate Ty Hamilton, now a basketball player at Scottsdale (Arizona) Community College, thinks Jake has understated his basketball talent.

"He did things I'm still amazed by," said Hamilton, now Jake's roommate at his Phoenix home. "I saw him score 32 points in basketball and play the whole game defending the other team's best player."

In baseball, he was an infielder with quick hands but not a big bat.

"I didn't spend enough time playing," Jake said. "I didn't play in the summer because I'd go visit my dad (who lived in Coeur d'Alene, Idaho)."

Jake gave up track when he reached high school. Earlier, he had done the long jump and high jump and some running events.

"I ran real well growing up," he said. "But there were days I just didn't like to run anymore. The last thing I ever did was run a 400. I couldn't stand it. It's the hardest run in the world—sprinting for a whole lap."

His high school football career began when, as a sophomore, he drove Boise Capital to a 96-yard score on his first possession.

In his final high school game, he marched Capital 80 yards in the final 90 seconds for the apparent tying touchdown against Pocatello High in the Idaho Class A1 title game. But Capital missed the extra point and lost, 14-13.

Jake still holds the Idaho state championship game record for punting average, 50 yards per kick.

He was a two-time all-state punter, as well as quarterback.

How good an athlete was Jake? Friends tell a story of how he once was late for a golf outing in Boise. He climbed out of his beat-up, old car wearing baggy, athletic shorts, his trademark baseball cap worn backwards and hightop sneakers with no laces.

He ran onto the first tee, saying hello and eating crackers. Jake then teed off—and hit the ball 330 yards down the middle of the fairway.

*Jake scores a touchdown against the Washington Redskins—
his first of three in the game. (AP/Wide World Photos)*

CHAPTER SIX

Worth the Trip

Arizona State football coach Bruce Snyder was not in a particularly good mood the January night in 1993 he showed up in Boise, Idaho, to recruit Jake. He had driven through snow and then, without boots, gloves or a topcoat—had to push a rented Cadillac driven by an assistant coach up a driveway and across a narrow wooden bridge.

"There was a foot of snow on the ground," Jake's mother said. "We live up a little hill and (Snyder) got stuck and had to get out and push the car."

Snyder thought the trip might have been a waste of time. Jake had told a Boise TV station he likely would go to Washington State.

"I'm 53, and I'm in this little hotel in Boise," Snyder said. "My feet are frozen. I've ruined a new, $300 pair of shoes. My pants are wet, and I've just gone to look at this skinny kid with long hair, not knowing if he was any good. I thought, 'What am I doing?'"

Snyder thought he made a good recruiting pitch. He brought with him a board game in which he compared ASU with Washington State in 12 categories, including weather and ability to win a national championship. In Snyder's mind, it was a no-brainer for Jake to pick the Sun Devils. Jake refused to commit at that time. He wanted to speak to his dad.

The coach still wasn't convinced that he had won over Jake. "I didn't think Jake was going to call me back," Snyder said. "I don't know if it was depression, but I was definitely taking an inventory of my life and my career."

Jake didn't wait long before making his recruiting decision. Thirty minutes after a frozen Snyder had left Jake's house, the quarterback called Snyder and told him he would attend ASU. Snyder didn't care if he needed new shoes.

Jake still had to make another phone call. He had to let Washington State Coach Mike Price know he was going to ASU. "He told me I made a mistake," Jake said. "Then, he hung up on me. I was 18 years old, pretty thin-skinned. Everything affected me."

As a junior at Arizona State, Jake threw for 2,222 yards. (Brian Spurlock)

The Sun Devils might have passed on Jake had Pat Barnes not turned them down to sign with California.

ASU wasn't Jake's first choice, either. He wanted to go to Stanford and had attended then-coach Bill Walsh's camp the previous summer. But Stanford quit recruiting Jake to sign Scott Frost, a Nebraska prep.

"(Jake) was a little surprised," Jake's mother said. "I think he thought playing for Bill Walsh would really be cool to do."

Four years later, Walsh, then working for the NFL's San Francisco 49ers, suggested the team draft Jake in the first round. They passed on him and instead selected Virginia Tech's Jim Druckenmiller.

***Jake dives across the goal line for a touchdown against
the Washington Redskins. (AP/Wide World Photos)***

First-Game Magic

Jake teased Juan Roque so much during their freshman year that the offensive lineman grabbed him by the throat one day and said, "I'm going to kill you."

The quarterback just laughed. "I knew he was crazy right then," Roque said.

Roque found out a lot more about Jake when he came off the bench his first game as a freshman and threw a 78-yard touchdown pass to wide receiver Carlos Artis on his first passing attempt.

So, in his first game in high school and college, he led his team to a score. It was to become a habit.

"I threw a duck up in the air and somehow the defensive back missed it," Jake said of the touchdown pass in his college debut.

He became a favorite of his ASU teammates, those same guys who questioned the Sun Devils' sanity for signing "a pencil neck who looks like a skate-board dude," as Roque once described Jake.

Wide receiver Keith Poole said when he met Jake for the first time, he wondered how the quarterback had even earned a scholarship. "He shows up, and here's this scrawny little guy with his baseball cap on backwards," Poole said. "Somebody told me, 'he's the quarterback,' and I thought we were in trouble."

Jake's first start came in game six against Oregon. The Sun Devils lost, but Jake was impressive, throwing two touchdown passes. He would start the next 36 games of his college career.

There were tough times the next two seasons. ASU went 3-8 and 6-5, respectively.

Jake had some great moments. As a sophomore, he became only the seventh player in school history to throw for more than 2,000 yards. A year later, he was picked first-team All-Pac 10 after throwing for 2,222 yards and 17 touchdowns.

Jake, whom ASU coaches called "Jimmy Stewart" for his aw-shucks personality, didn't think the honors were any big deal.

"I had all his awards up in his room, like a shrine," his mother said. "But when he came home after his sophomore year, he told me to take them down and put them in a trunk.

"The only thing he wanted left on the walls was an article from *Handball Magazine* (April, 1993) entitled, 'The Four Horseman of Boise.' It's about Jake, his dad and brothers when they played in the Boise Open handball tournament.

Much was expected of Jake heading into his senior year, but those expectations were in Tempe, not the rest of the country. Jake wasn't even on the Heisman Trophy ballot when the season began.

People around the nation began to notice when Jake threw for 292 yards and a touchdown to beat top-ranked Nebraska, 19-0, ending the country's longest winning streak.

The Huskers had won 26 consecutive games and 37 in a row during the regular season and had won back-to-back national crowns. They had not been shut out in 23 years.

After that game, Jake's life changed. For the longest time, he could walk around campus unnoticed. Now, everyone wanted a piece of Jake.

In fact, in the week after the Nebraska win, Arizona State's sports information office had 146 interview requests for him.

ASU officials also sat Jake down and asked him if he were prepared to be a Heisman candidate. Jake thought they were joking.

"A couple of years ago, no one knew me," Jake said at the time. "I'm in this (place) and two girls come up to my buddy, and he tells them he's on the football team. They asked, 'Oh, do you know Jake Plummer?' And he goes, 'That's him right there.' They said, 'No, you're not. You're not him.'

"But now my face is all over the place. You got to be from out of town not to know."

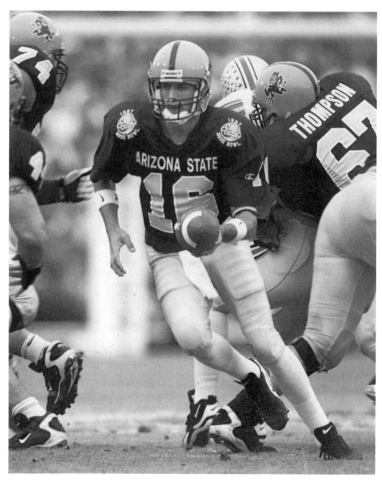

Jake runs a play against Ohio State in the 1997 Rose Bowl. (AP/Wide World Photos)

CHAPTER EIGHT

Coming Up Roses

Midway through Jake's senior season, everyone in the Valley of the Sun was talking about ASU's chances of going to the Rose Bowl.

His brothers were worried that Jake might get cocky.

"Aw, shut up, Wuerffel's better than you," Brett said of University of Florida quarterback Danny Wuerffel.

Jake got another dose of reality when a week after the Nebraska victory, his car was stolen. It wasn't a luxury car. It was a red Jeep Cherokee that always was filled with golf clubs, golf balls, CD's, tapes, jock straps and shoes.

"I'm surprised there were no hamsters," Roque said.

When Jake went to pick up the towed car, his buddy's vehicle broke down in the 100-degree heat. Jake was stranded but humbled.

The rest of the season went much better. He led the Sun Devils back from a 28-7 deficit at UCLA, putting the team ahead with a 16-yard touchdown catch. Not pass. Catch. It came on a halfback pass from J.R. Redmond.

Jake caught the pass on the 10-yard line and slithered like a snake into the end zone.

"I get a lot of kidding about my moves," Jake said. "I probably looked pretty funny with my skinny legs, looking like a chicken."

In the fourth quarter alone, with the Sun Devils still trailing, 34-21, Jake threw a touchdown pass, caught a score and ran for one.

"When I'm old and retired and not playing football anymore, I'll get out that UCLA tape and enjoy the fourth quarter," Jake said.

The next week, ASU trailed Southern Cal, 14-0, before Jake rallied them to an overtime victory. "Our Rose Bowl year, we knew if we needed points, he was going to get them," said Pat Tillman, a linebacker for the Sun Devils who plays safety on the Cardinals. "If we had any chance, he'd get it done."

USC Coach John Robinson was in such awe, he called Jake a "Joe Montana-style quarterback."

"Maybe he was a little distraught from the game, and he didn't know what he was saying," Jake said. "It means I'm small and wiry."

Snake-fever was catching. When the Cardinals came from behind to win, their quarterback, Boomer Esiason, said, "I pulled a Jake Plummer."

Jake works out at his first Cardinals mini-camp.
(AP/Wide World Photos)

ASU clinched its first Rose Bowl berth in 10 years with a 35-7 victory over California. Sun Devils fans were so excited, they tore down the goalposts and carried them down Mill Avenue in downtown Tempe, chanting, "Rose Bowl."

Two days later, Jake walked into a sociology class and got a standing ovation.

*Jake (center, with his family) finished third in the
1996 Heisman Trophy voting. (Marilyn Plummer)*

CHAPTER NINE

New York, New York

Still remaining was the Heisman vote. Jake was a longshot even though the numbers gave him a chance. He threw for 2,575 yards and 23 touchdowns his senior year.

The Sun Devils were 11-0 and No. 2 in the nation and headed for a Rose Bowl game against Big Ten champion Ohio State.

As Jake prepared for his trip to New York's Downtown Athletic Club for the Heisman ceremony, his mom insisted he wear a suit. Jake told her he had a sport coat, but that was one argument he wouldn't win.

Jake was asked if his suit was an Armani. He didn't know. "Just as long as the top matches the bottom," Jake said.

He finished third in the Heisman balloting behind Wuerffel and Iowa State running back Troy Davis. But Jake wasn't disappointed. He was driven around in limousines, treated like royalty.

"To get to shake Earl Campbell's hand, that was big time," said Jake, who also met Archie Griffin and Army's Glenn Davis, the Heisman winner 50 years ago.

"That was big time. It's hard to explain how it makes you feel. In 30 years, I could be nobody, but I can always say I was a part of this."

Meanwhile, his dad and two brothers played handball at 3 a.m. at the Downtown Athletic Club. Idaho would have been proud.

In 1997, Jake set the Cardinals' rookie passing record with 2,203 yards. (Joe Robbins)

There also was a trip to Rockefeller Center, home of the world's biggest Christmas tree. Jake took a disposable camera out of his pocket and started clicking.

"I just wanted to get a shot of my mom with the Christmas tree behind her," Jake said.

A few weeks later, Jake ended his ASU career in the Rose Bowl. He continued his flair for the dramatic.

Jake scored on an 11-yard run with 1:40 remaining to give the Sun Devils a 17-14 lead. But then he stood on the sidelines and watched the Buckeyes drive 65 yards in 12 plays and score with 19 seconds remaining to win.

Ohio State sophomore wide receiver David Boston scored the game-winner on a five-yard touchdown catch. Boston was asked later what opposing athlete he admired the most. He said it was Jake.

Boston, the Cardinals' 1999 top draft pick, had no idea at the time that someday he and Jake would be teammates.

Jake was drafted by the Cardinals in 1997. (Joe Robbins)

CHAPTER TEN

Sleepwalking

At first, Cardinals Coach Vince Tobin wasn't wild about picking Jake, the Arizona State product, in the second round of the 1997 draft.

He was worried that it would put too much pressure on starter Kent Graham, that whenever Graham faltered, the fans would call for Jake.

Other teams weren't completely sold on Jake. "If I had a late second-round pick, I'd take him," one NFL personnel boss said. "If you want to nitpick, maybe he lacks size, maybe he doesn't have a great arm to throw long. Maybe he doesn't throw a tight spiral on every play. Maybe he's too skinny, and you don't like the way he pulls his socks up to his knees. But he's a competitive playmaker, and that's all you want."

The draft experts also had doubts. ESPN's Mel Kiper didn't list him in his top 60 players.

Then, there was Jake's performance at the NFL's Indianapolis scouting combine. There was nothing wrong with the way he threw the ball. It's just when Jake stripped down to his shorts and scouts saw his 6 foot 2, 192-pound bony body, they couldn't dream of taking him in the first round.

The Cardinals didn't enter the draft confident they would get Jake with the 11th pick overall in the second round. Walsh, working as a consultant for the 49ers, recommended they take Jake in the first round. They didn't listen to Walsh and took Druckenmiller instead.

As the second round began, the Cardinals still didn't know if they would have a chance to pick a hero in the Valley of the Sun. Atlanta, looking for a quarterback, had two second-round picks before the Cardinals' choice. St. Louis also thought long and hard about taking him.

A few days before the draft, Tobin met with Jake and talked to him about the pressure everyone would be under if he became a Cardinal.

"One of the things we were concerned about was whether there would be too much pressure on Jake to perform too early or too much pressure on us to play him too early," Tobin said.

The Cardinals' fears were over as soon as they spoke with Jake. When he was available in the second round, they didn't hesitate to take him—once they found him.

He was taking a nap in his suite at the Biltmore Hotel in Phoenix, tired from a day of golf and swimming.

Finally, a friend tapped Jake on the shoulder and said, "Wake up. You're an Arizona Cardinal."

Jake thought he was dreaming.

Stink Bomb

Early in Jake's first training camp, Larry Centers and several of his teammates spotted a maimed, baby skunk in the middle of the road. They quickly slammed on the brakes and got out of their cars.

Suddenly, the light went on in several players' minds.

"You think we could get Jake?"

"Nah."

"You bet."

"Centers said it was a small skunk and didn't have any stink," punter Jeff Feagles said. "Like he's Mr. Wilderness."

Feagles then grabbed a golf club, a 4-iron, out of his car and scooped up the skunk. "They were going to use a driver, but it was too much," Feagles said.

The players drove to the dormitory at Northern Arizona University, where Centers handed Jake a bag with the skunk inside.

Jake dropped the sack into a dumpster but then retrieved it after Centers shouted at him, "Hey, rook, what are you doing. There's chicken wings inside that bag. That's our food. Get it out."

Jake took the bag to his room. Seconds later, the skunk was out of the bag and near his bed. "I got scared, real scared," Jake said. "I didn't want to get sprayed and have to be secluded or banned from the team because I stunk so bad. I just turned around and got out quick.

He ran out of his room into the hallway, where Kent Graham was waiting for him, video camera in hand. "I've reviewed the tape and I feel pretty comfortable it's going to be up for an Emmy," Graham said.

Jake then called security, which took the skunk away in a trash can. Before leaving, the security officer asked Jake how the skunk got into his room.

"I brought it in," Jake told him.

He heard about it for several days. He also scored big points with his teammates for being able to laugh it off.

"I was just a dumb rookie," Jake said. "I fell for a big trick.

"I could have retaliated, but it would just get worse for me. The next thing I know, I might have a half-dead elk in my room."

Jake scrambles with the ball during a practice at training camp. (AP/Wide World Photos)

Destiny

Jake was listed as fourth team at the start of his first Cardinals' training camp. He didn't move up the depth chart after his first preseason game. It was a disaster. He completed only five of 16 passes for 52 yards in the 1997 preseason opener at Seattle. He also was sacked once and threw an interception.

Still, it was better than Jake looked some days in practice.

"I was shaky," he said. "I didn't know what was going on. I'd (drop back) and start running right away. I had no patience. I was confused.

"I was real frustrated at camp. I would drop the snap and have (former offensive line coach Carl) Mauck yell at me. It was no fun."

One day during camp, Jake was so frustrated as he sat down and talked to teammate Frank Sanders that he became emotional. He questioned whether he was good enough.

Sanders gave him a short pep talk and told him to just sit back and relax.

Jake did nothing but sit until starter Kent Graham suffered a sprained knee against the New York Giants in week seven. Suddenly, Jake wasn't the scout team quarterback anymore. He was the backup to Stoney Case.

Case was pulled after three quarters of his first NFL start the next week at Philadelphia and replaced by Jake. As soon as Jake ran into the huddle, everything changed for the Cardinals.

First, Jake told his teammates there would be no more goofing around. "Then, he announces, 'We're going to take this down and score,'" center Mike Devlin said.

The more the veterans thought about Jake's remarks, they liked it. "We needed something," offensive tackle Lomas Brown said. "We were at the point of being desperate. We needed any spark."

Wide receiver Rob Moore listened to Jake in the huddle and then smiled. "He came into the huddle jacked up and was yelling a whole bunch of stuff," Moore said. "He believed we could take it down and score, and we needed that (attitude)."

Jake wasn't nervous about his pro debut. But he didn't expect to start on his own two-yard line. "It was kind of amazing, I was actually getting a shot," he said. "It didn't really sink in until after-

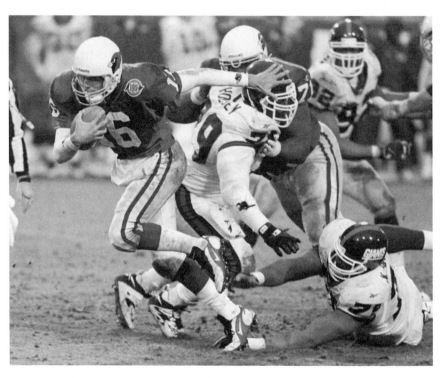

***Jake scrambles against the New York Giants in 1998.
(AP/Wide World Photos)***

wards. But I just had to go out and play. We were down to our third (quarterback), and no one was really expecting much from me."

Fourteen plays later, Jake's first possession ended with wide receiver Kevin Williams running a slant pattern. Williams caught the pass at the 25 and outraced two defenders into the end zone for a 31-yard score and a brief lead.

Bob Ferguson, vice president/player personnel of the Cardinals, got emotional in the press box at Veterans Stadium. He said in meetings before the 1997 draft that Jake had a chance to be a special player because of his comeback ability. He remembers talking about Jake in one meeting for 35 minutes.

"I was excited because that was the kind of thing we hoped he could do on a regular basis," Ferguson said. "It was storybook, but the ending can be storybook, too.

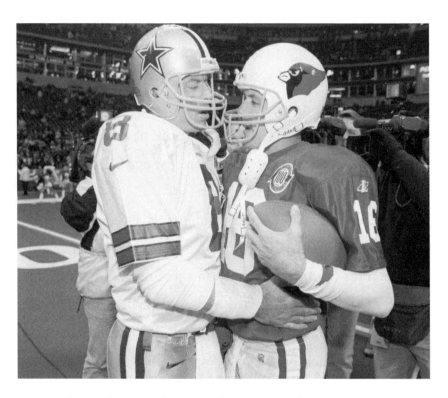

***Jake and Troy Aikman embrace after the Cardinals
defeated the Cowboys in the 1999 NFC Wild Card
game in Texas. (AP/Wide World Photos)***

"I know there were some questions about this kid (physically). But everybody said a horse (Seattle Slew) was too short. But all he did was win the Triple Crown."

The rest of Jake's rookie year didn't go as well. Tobin named him the starter the next week against Tennessee, an announcement so big that two Phoenix radio stations carried it live. In the 48 hours after Tobin's announcement, more than 3,000 tickets were sold.

"Jake mania," Jake's agent, Leigh Steinberg, called it.

Then, it poured on his first practice as a starter. "It rained to prove that Jake can walk on water," one practice observer said.

At 22 years, 10 months, Jake would become the franchise's second-youngest starting quarterback since 1960. At least, he didn't line up behind guard as Dallas' Troy Aikman and New England's Drew Bledsoe did.

In Jake's starting debut, he was intercepted four times and sacked six times in a 41-14 loss to Tennessee. "I did plenty wrong," Jake said. "It was ugly."

The fans at Sun Devil Stadium didn't care. They cheered him every time he ran onto the field. In fact, he got a standing ovation after going three-and-out in his first series.

A few weeks later, Jake was benched late in a home game against Philadelphia, and the fans booed. It didn't matter that Graham came into the game and helped the Cardinals break a six-game losing streak. One talk-radio caller even said she would rather the Cardinals lose with Jake than win with Graham. "That's crazy," Jake said.

Jake won only two games his rookie season, beating Baltimore, 16-13, and Atlanta, 29-26, in the season finale as the team finished 4-12. But he also set an NFL rookie record when he threw for 388 yards against the New York Giants.

His four touchdown passes against Washington set a team mark, and after the game, Redskins Coach Norv Turner told Tobin he had a special player in Jake.

The season ended with Jake driving the Cardinals 80 yards in 12 plays to beat Atlanta. He threw the game-winning touchdown pass with five seconds left and than added the two-point conversion.

Until that drive, Jake hadn't completed a pass in the second half. "He's 'The Man,'" Moore said. "Some guys know how to get it done. You can be lousy the whole game and then, when it's time to win, get that spark."

As Jake was about to leave the locker room, Sanders stopped him and told him to listen. The fans were chanting, "Jake, Jake, Jake."

A Cardinals assistant then turned to a reporter and said, "You're going to have fun watching that kid grow up."

Comeback Kid

Talk about pressure. Before Jake had taken a snap in 1998, Walsh was predicting the second-year pro could be the NFL's Most Valuable Player.

"Barring the unforeseen injury, and providing he someday has a supporting cast and system that can allow him to flourish, I see Jake having a Montana-like career, including the Super Bowls," Walsh told *Sports Illustrated*.

Jake was one of five Cardinals captains in 1998.
(Joe Robbins)

If that weren't enough of a load, the NFL's Internet site asked fans who would be the league's breakthrough player in 1998, and Jake was the overwhelming winner, getting 19.9 percent of the 3,338 votes.

And his teammates voted Jake one of five team captains, ignoring the fact that he had played in only 10 regular-season games. So Jake was being asked not only to lead the Cardinals to their first winning season since 1984 but also to carry a franchise on his back.

"One rookie year doesn't mean I'll be the next Joe Montana," Jake said. "Maybe I'll be the first Jake Plummer."

The start of Jake's season was forgettable. He was sacked twice and lost a fumble in a lopsided defeat at Dallas in the opener. A week later, he was intercepted three times and sacked seven times in another blowout loss at Seattle. After he had a sec-

*Artie Smith of the Cowboys attempts to tackle "The Snake."
(AP/Wide World Photos)*

ond-quarter melt-down against Oakland on September 4—one interception was returned for a touchdown and another was returned to the Cardinals' four—some suggested he should be benched.

Everything changed for Jake after the team's open date in late October. He had a better understanding of the team's complicated "West Coast" offense and it showed.

He took the Cardinals 50 yards in five plays and 27 seconds to beat the Washington Redskins, 29-27, on Joe Nedney's 47-yard field goal with two seconds left.

"Everyone believed," Jake said. "Even with 30 seconds left, I kept yelling, 'We can do this. We can do this.' And we responded."

Afterwards, he was greeted by Robinson, the former USC coach. "You looked like you were playing us," Robinson told him.

Robinson then added that Jake was all about intangibles. "You can't measure them. But some people have them. And Jake always seems to get it done at the end."

In the second half, he completed 16 of 17 passes, including 15 in a row, a franchise record. "I'm very proud of him," offensive coordinator Marc Trestman said. "We know he's special. We also knew it was just a matter of time before he's unleashed."

The Washington victory was Jake's sixth come-from-behind or "game saving" performance in his first 19 games, something Denver's John Elway, Miami's Dan Marino, Buffalo's Jim Kelly and even Montana didn't accomplish.

"My mom and my family keep telling me it's getting tough on them," Jake said. "My mom says she can't take it. It's too hard on her heart.

"But I love it. It's do-or-die. You either succeed or you lose right there. There's nothing more exciting, but you don't want to have to do it all the time."

Jake was far from finished. He would rally the Cardinals from a 28-0 deficit against Dallas. The team, trailing by seven points, had the ball on the Cowboys' five-yard line with 11 seconds left. On the final play of the game, Jake threw a pass to Moore in the end zone, with Cowboys cornerback Kevin Smith draped all over him. Replays showed it was an obvious pass interference call, but no flags were thrown, and the Cowboys held on for the win.

He finished with 465 yards passing, the third best mark in the team's 100 seasons. It also was the second most by a Cowboys' opponent.

During the Cardinals' stretch run for the play-offs, Jake kept leading them to heart-stopping wins. In the final three possessions of a 20-17 overtime win at Philadelphia, Jake drove the Cardinals 66 yards in 10 plays to tie the game, positioned them at the Eagles' 17-yard line for a missed 34-yard field goal attempt and marched them 58 yards to the

Eagles' 14-yard line for kicker Chris Jacke's game-winning field goal in overtime.

Opponents had seen nothing yet.

The next week, the Cardinals trailed New Orleans, 17-16, with 1:21 left and took over on their eight-yard line.

No sweat. Jake drove them 73 yards in six plays to win on Jacke's fourth field goal of the game with no time remaining.

Signs at Sun Devil Stadium celebrated:

"PLUMMER 3:16."

"ON THE EIGHTH DAY, GOD CREATED JAKE."

"WE BELIEVE."

A day after the New Orleans win, the Cardinals gave Jake the biggest signing bonus in NFL history ($15 million) with a four-year contract extension. Then, he went out and celebrated by helping them to a 16-13 victory over the San Diego Chargers in the regular-season finale, sending the Cardinals to the playoffs for the first time since 1982.

They won at Dallas in the wild-card round, their first victory there since 1989 and the franchise's first playoff win since 1947. Their best season in Arizona ended the next week with a loss at Minnesota.

Jake finished with nine comeback wins in his first 25 starts. He was a hero and a rich man.

Money hadn't changed Jake. In fact, minutes after Jake signed the new deal, his dad, Steve, laughed as he thought about his son's first car, a yellow 1968 Hornet, which had a door missing.

Jake also drove a 1974 Dodge Dart, a car known as the "Green Weenie." The shock absorbers were so worn, when the car turned the corner, it leaned to one side.

"Jake never cared what he drove," his dad said.

That's why at ASU he had a Mazda with no air conditioning. It wasn't a pretty sight on the days the temperature broke 110.

"Heck, I didn't care," Jake said. "Rubber wheels were better than rubber heels."

Jake Plummer Quick Facts

Full Name: Jason Steve Plummer

Team: Arizona Cardinals

Position: Quarterback

Number: 16

Height, weight: 6-2, 197

Birthdate: December 19, 1974

Hometown: Boise, Idaho

Years in the league: 2

Drafted: Second round (42nd overall)

College: Arizona State

1998 Highlights: Fourth in the NFL in passing yardage, completing 324 passes for 3,727 yards.

Statistical Highlight: Set Cardinal rookie passing records in 1997 by completing 157 passes for 2,203 yards and 15 touchdowns.

Little-Known Fact: Plummer threw his first NFL pass to himself when he caught a batted pass.

Jake Plummer Statistics

1998 Regular Season Passing

Date	Opp.	W/L	Comp.	Att.	Yds.	TD	Int.	LG
Sep. 6	@Dal	L	14	33	166	0	0	41
Sep. 13	@Sea	L	22	36	204	1	3	23
Sep. 20	Phi	W	21	35	137	1	0	26
Sep. 27	@StL	W	21	31	211	1	1	29
Oct. 4	Oak	L	23	39	208	2	3	23
Oct. 11	Chi	W	18	25	157	0	2	24
Oct. 18	@NYN	L	12	21	139	1	2	25
Nov. 1	@Det	W	15	25	198	2	1	36
Nov. 8	Was	W	22	30	186	1	0	18
Nov. 15	Dal	L	31	56	465	3	1	57
Nov. 22	@Was	W	17	28	251	2	1	40
Nov. 29	@KC	L	20	37	250	1	2	40
Dec. 6	NYN	L	18	40	263	1	2	54

Date	Opp.	W/L	Comp.	Att.	Yds.	TD	Int.	LG
Dec. 13	@Phi	W	18	26	234	1	1	30
Dec. 20	NO	W	32	44	394	0	1	33
Dec. 27	SD	W	20	41	274	0	0	36
Total		9-7	324	547	3,737	17	20	57

1998 Regular Season Rushing

Date	Opp.	W/L	Att.	Yds.	Avg.	TD	LG
Sep. 6	@Dal	L	3	8	2.7	1	6
Sep. 13	@Sea	L	3	23	7.7	0	11
Sep. 20	Phi	W	2	5	2.5	0	3
Sep. 27	@StL	W	6	10	1.7	0	8
Oct. 4	Oak	L	2	11	5.5	0	8
Oct. 11	Chi	W	4	8	2.0	0	6
Oct. 18	@NYN	L	2	8	4.0	0	7
Nov. 1	@Det	W	5	-3	-.6	0	1
Nov. 8	Was	W	3	50	16.7	0	27
Nov. 15	Dal	L	3	6	2.0	0	4
Nov. 22	@Was	W	6	10	1.7	3	10
Nov. 29	@KC	L	1	8	8.0	0	8
Dec. 6	NYN	L	4	18	4.5	0	11
Dec. 13	@Phi	W	3	17	5.7	0	14
Dec. 20	NO	W	4	38	9.5	0	31
Dec. 27	SD	W	0	0	—	0	0
Total		9-7	51	217	4.3	4	27

1998 Regular Season Leaders
Passing Yardage

1.	Brett Favre	Green Bay Packers	4,212
2.	Steve Young	San Francisco 49ers	4,170
3.	Peyton Manning	Indianapolis Colts	3,739
4.	**JAKE PLUMMER**	**ARIZONA CARDINALS**	**3,737**
5.	Randall Cunningham	Minnesota Vikings	3,704
6.	Drew Bledsoe	New England Patriots	3,633
7.	Dan Marino	Miami Dolphins	3,497
8.	Trent Green	Washington Redskins	3,441
9.	Vinny Testaverde	New York Jets	3,256
10.	Steve McNair	Tennessee Oilers	3,228
11.	Chris Chandler	Atlanta Falcons	3,154
12.	John Elway	Denver Broncos	2,806
13.	Trent Dilfer	Tampa Bay Buccaneers	2,729
14.	Doug Flutie	Buffalo Bills	2,711
15.	Steve Beuerlein	Carolina Panthers	2,613
16.	Mark Brunell	Jacksonville Jaguars	2,601
17.	Kordell Stewart	Pittsburgh Steelers	2,560
18.	Tony Banks	St. Louis Rams	2,535
19.	Troy Aikman	Dallas Cowboys	2,330
20.	Rich Gannon	Kansas City Chiefs	2,305

Baseball Superstar Series Titles

Collect Them All!

___ Mark McGwire: Mac Attack!

___ #1 *Derek Jeter: The Yankee Kid*

___ #2 *Ken Griffey Jr.: The Home Run Kid*

___ #3 *Randy Johnson: Arizona Heat!*

___ #4 *Sammy Sosa: Slammin' Sammy*

___ #5 *Bernie Williams: Quiet Superstar*

___ #6 *Omar Vizquel: The Man with the Golden Glove*

___ #7 *Mo Vaughn: Angel on a Mission*

___ #8 *Pedro Martinez: Throwing Strikes*

___ #9 *Juan Gonzalez: Juan Gone!*

___ #10 *Tony Gwynn: Mr. Padre*

___ #11 *Kevin Brown: Kevin with a "K"*

___ #12 *Mike Piazza: Mike and the Mets*

___ #13 *Larry Walker: Canadian Rocky*

___ #14 *Nomar Garciaparra: High 5!*

___ #15 *Sandy and Roberto Alomar: Baseball Brothers*

___ #16 *Mark Grace: Winning with Grace*

___ #17 *Curt Schilling: Phillie Phire!*

___ #18 *Alex Rodriguez: A+ Shortstop*

___ #19 *Roger Clemens: Rocket!*

Only $4.95 per book!

Football Superstar Series Titles
Collect Them All!

Only $4.95 per book!

Basketball Superstar Series Titles

Collect Them All!

___ #1 *Kobe Bryant: The Hollywood Kid*

___ #2 *Keith Van Horn: Nothing But Net*

___ #3 *Antoine Walker: Kentucky Celtic*

___ #4 *Kevin Garnett: Scratching the Surface*

___ #5 *Tim Duncan: Slam Duncan*

___ #6 *Reggie Miller: From Downtown*

___ #7 *Jason Kidd: Rising Sun*

___ #8 *Vince Carter: Air Canada*

Only $4.95 per book!

Hockey Superstar Series Titles

Collect Them All!

___ #1 *John LeClair: Flying High*

___ #2 *Mike Richter: Gotham Goalie*

___ #3 *Paul Kariya: Maine Man*

___ #4 *Dominik Hasek: The Dominator*

___ #5 *Jaromir Jagr: Czechmate*

___ #6 *Martin Brodeur: Picture Perfect*

___ #8 *Ray Bourque: Bruins Legend*

Only $4.95 per book!

Call Toll Free: 1-877-424-BOOK (2665) or visit us at www.sportspublishinginc.com